W9-AJP-649

National Parks

by Lisa Trumbauer

Consultant: Steve Dodd, Director, Park Ranger Training Program, Northern Arizona Uinversity

Yellow
Umbrella
Books
for early readers

Yellow Umbrella Books are published by Red Brick Learning
7825 Telegraph Road, Bloomington, Minnesota 55438
http://www.redbricklearning.com

Editorial Director: Mary Lindeen
Senior Editor: Hollie J. Endres
Senior Designer: Gene Bentdahl
Photo Researcher: Signature Design
Developer: Raindrop Publishing
Consultant: Steve Dodd, Director, Park Ranger Training Program, Northern Arizona Uinversity
Conversion Assistants: Jenny Marks, Laura Manthe

Library of Congress Cataloging-in-Publication Data
Trumbauer, Lisa, 1963-
  National Parks / by Lisa Trumbauer
     p. cm.
  Includes index.
  ISBN 0-7368-5848-2 (hardcover)
  ISBN 0-7368-5278-6 (softcover)
  1. National parks and reserves—United States—Juvenile literature. 2. United States—History,
Local—Juvenile literature. I. Title.
  E160.T78 2005
  333.78'3'0973—dc22
                                                    2005015623

Photo Credits:
Cover and Title Page: Corbis; Pages 2–4: Comstock Photos; Pages 5 and 6: Corel; Page 7:
AP/Wide World Photos; Page 8: Corbis; Page 9: Corel; Page 10: Image Ideas; Page 11: David
Muench/Corbis; Page 12: Corbis; Page 13: Jeff Barnard/AP/Wide World Photos; Page 14: Brian
Cassey/AP/Wide World Photos

1 2 3 4 5 6 11 10 09 08 07 06

Table of Contents

Natural Beauty

Yellowstone National Park in Wyoming is a place of great **natural** beauty. It has mountains and lakes. It has **bison** and elk. It has a **geyser** called Old Faithful.

National parks **protect** the natural beauty of the United States. Yellowstone was the first area to be made a national park. That means that the land is protected by the government. Let's visit some of our other national parks.

A Land of Contrasts

Natural beauty differs from place to place. Death Valley National Park is in California. It's a hot, dry desert. Few plants or animals live here.

Everglades National Park in Florida is full of plants and animals. More than 300 kinds of birds live here, as well as 700 plant **species**. Visitors might also see alligators or manatees.

Amazing Mountains

The tallest mountain in North America is in Denali National Park in Alaska. It's Mount McKinley, and many people try to climb the mountain each year. Half of the climbers can make it all the way to the top.

Great Smoky Mountains National Park, in Tennessee and North Carolina, has mountains that are more soft and rolling. "The Smokies" are some of the oldest mountains in the world.

Fantastic Forests

Many forests have been protected as national parks. Redwood National Park was set up to protect the redwood trees of northern California. Redwoods are among the largest trees on Earth.

In the fall, the forests of Shenandoah National Park in Virginia are bursting with color. The leaves turn beautiful shades of red, orange, and yellow. Many visitors to the park enjoy the view from Skyline Drive. This road travels along the tops of the mountains that make up this national park.

Canyons and Caves

Grand Canyon National Park is in Arizona. The canyon's walls are striped with color. The colors come from the different layers of rock that make up the canyon. The Grand Canyon is one mile (1.61 kilometers) deep!

In Kentucky, an amazing world of caves exists below ground. They make up Mammoth Cave National Park. The cave tunnels are about 350 miles (563 kilometers) long! It is the world's largest cave **system**.

Lava, Lakes, and Lots More

Long ago, volcanoes formed the islands that are now called Hawaii. Today, some volcanoes in Hawaii are still active. They burst with fiery lava and steam. Visitors can see them at Hawaii Volcanoes National Park.

Crater Lake National Park, in Oregon, has the deepest lake in the United States—1,900 feet (579 meters) deep. The lake formed in the mouth of a **dormant** volcano. Scientists think the volcano erupted about 7,000 years ago.

On the other side of the United States you will find shipwrecks and the coral reefs of Biscayne National Park, in Florida. This park is yet another example of the different kinds of natural beauty and history protected by our national park system.

Glossary

bison—a large hairy mammal similar to a buffalo

dormant—not active, resting

geyser—a hole in the earth through which hot water and steam shoot up periodically

natural—found in nature or made by nature

protect—to keep something safe from harm

species—a group of plants or animals that are similar or the same in certain ways

system—things that exist together or work together in an organized way

Index

Word Count: 453
Early-Intervention Level: L